WELCOME

TAROT
THE MINI COURSE METHOD
Bootcamp

By your instructor
Stephanie Roberts
(who has DONE it for herself with the Tarot as her best friend!)

ISBN: 978-1-7638221-1-5

Facebook:
https://www.facebook.com/StephanieRobertsTeacher
https://www.facebook.com/StephanieRobertsWriter
https://www.facebook.com/StephanieRobertsAuthor/

Website:
https://stephanieroberts.college

Udemy:
https://www.udemy.com/user/stephanie-roberts-18/

WELCOME

GAIN INSIGHT TO READ TAROT FOR YOURSELF IN 5 DAYS

A mini method Bootcamp designed to deliver BIG results in reading Tarot for YOURSELF in just 5 days!

Welcome to the Tarot Mini–Course Bootcamp. I am so happy to have you on this journey with me!

My mission and my vision is to help like-minded people achieve their goals and create a fulfilled life as I have with the Tarot as my guide and friend.

I am now down the track of thirty years of creating my life with the Tarot, so I can speak from my own life experience!

My Name is
Stephanie Roberts

- Tarot Teacher, Reader and Advisor
- Reiki Master
- Certified Counsellor
- Business Owner of training colleges
- Author
- Screenwriter
- Artist
- Wife, Mother & Grandmother (My proudest role)

If you don't know who I am – my name is Stephanie Roberts. I have been reading Tarot for myself for over thirty years to create my life with the guidance of the magic of the Tarot. I have also read for many others, and you may go on to do so yourself. But for the purpose of this mini course, we are going to concentrate on you first.

When you help yourself, you can then help others.

My career has spanned over a decade with the Tarot guiding me to create the many facets of my life as an artist, screenwriter, author, business owner of training colleges, counsellor, Reiki master, Tarot teacher and advisor and my proudest role of wife, mother and grandmother of two sons and five grandsons!

In the last chapter of my life (as a writer I tend to read my life in chapters) my vision and mission is to help as many women reach a happy and successful life in their careers, relationships and personal growth as I have. It is very doable with trusting yourself, your intuition, and the Tarot as your friend.

Relationships

Love Trust Honesty Respect Kindness Communication

Most of the questions I get asked are on relationships. More so in this ever changing modern world than back when I was courting and married in the late sixties. That would be me riding on the pillion of my boyfriend's bike (now my husband). Picnics on the grass on a Sunday morning. The world was our oyster without a care!

Life is more complicated today.

However, the basics of a good relationship remain the same. Love. Trust. Honesty. Respect. Kindness and good Communication. Over the many years as we mature in our relationship, if we don't grow together, we won't stay together.

Change is the only constant thing in life. Be prepared to change and watch your life evolve in leaps and bounds with the guidance of your true friend the TAROT.

I am going to show you how. This is my way, but you will develop ways to unfold your own life with the Tarot, when you make a connection with your best friend.

Nothing is set in stone. Be creative and develop your creativity once you learn the basics of anything in life. I have, and I am happy as to where it has got me today.

Here you will gain insight to read Tarot for yourself in 5 days! Yes, just 5 days!

This is a truly mini course with big results for you to create a life of fulfillment and joy! Most of us want to achieve results fast; not have to study for 12 months or more to get started. So here we are going to work together to get results fast.

There are many courses on reading Tarot and Tarot readers all have their own style of reading for their clients. This course is different.

If you have never seen a Tarot deck of cards. Get yourself one. We are working with the Rider Waite deck here. I suggest you start with this deck as you work with me.

This mini course is about teaching you to let the Tarot cards guide you on your journey of love, career, and pathway of life.

I am a firm believer that we create our own destiny. The future is not set in stone. Our past and present govern our future outcomes. We can change what we want in life if we pay heed to the messages of the cards, address our weaknesses, and move on from past hurt and pain.

Stephanie Marie

Author and Tarot Advisor
Enkindle Publishing
Creator of "Intuitive Tarot for Women" a Simple Mini Course

Facebook:
https://www.facebook.com/StephanieRobertsTeacher
https://www.facebook.com/StephanieRobertsWriter
https://www.facebook.com/StephanieRobertsAuthor/

Website:
https://stephanieroberts.college

Udemy:
https://www.udemy.com/user/stephanie-roberts-18/

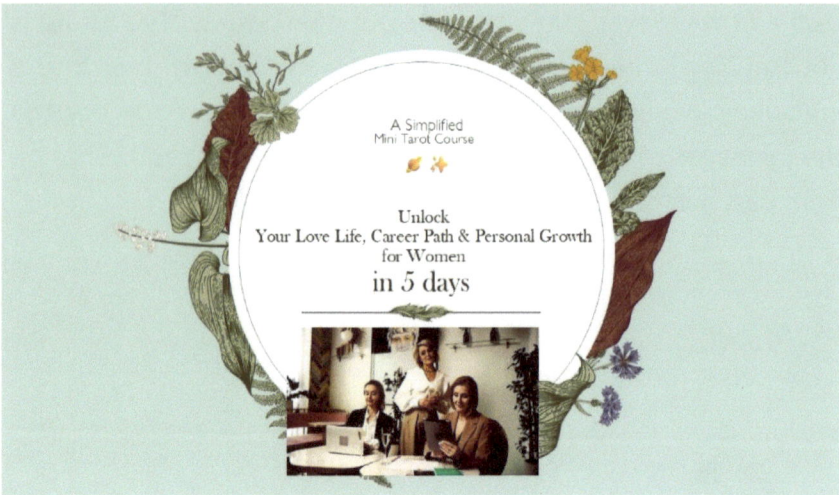

A Simplified
Mini Tarot Course

Unlock
Your Love Life, Career Path & Personal Growth
for Women
in 5 days

It is an amazing and exciting journey to unlock YOUR love life, career path and personal growth.

As my student of this course, you will have access to my email contact to continue working with me on your journey of learning to let the Tarot guide you on your life path.

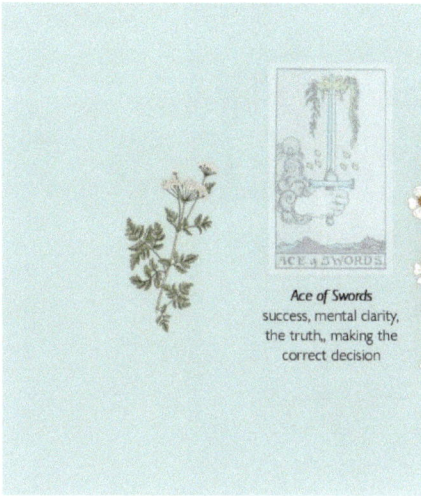

Roadmap

- Introduction
- Technique
- Process
- Intuition
- Formula
- Mastery

Here is the Roadmap you will follow with me to Mastery!

- Day 1
  Will cover Introduction and Technique
- Day 2
  Will cover the Process
- Day 3
  Intuition the root of successfully reading Tarot for yourself
- Day 4
  My unique Formula
- Day 5
  Mastery – yes you will master reading YOUR cards simply and quickly

Introduction and Technique

ENKINDLE
PUBLISHING

So, let's start with the Introduction and Technique! Come with me, you are in for quite a RIDE!

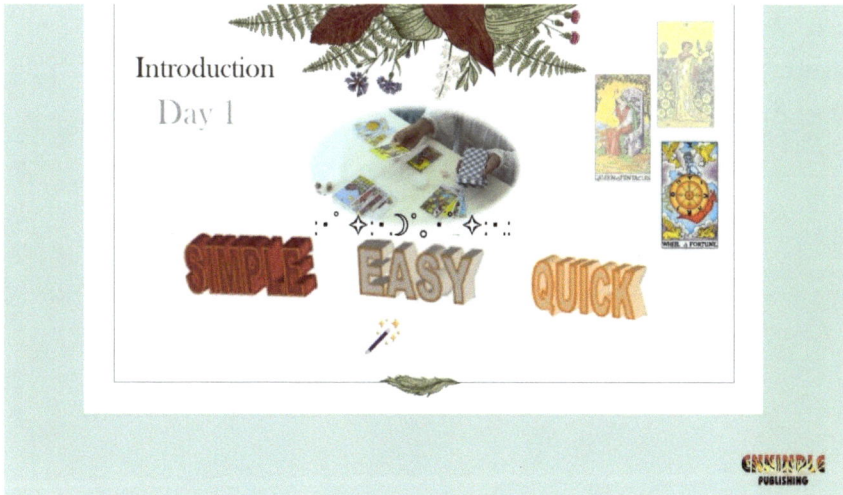

Introduction
Day 1

SIMPLE EASY QUICK

This mini course is Simple, Easy and Quick! It will teach you all the basics to get you reading your life successfully and more so leading your life the way you desire. I have been a teacher of many subjects in my life, but I never teach anything without having done it successfully for myself.

Doing something is good – getting results is vital! Yes, I did all the many motivational and spiritual courses of the great teachers of our time - Louise Hay, Doreen Virtue, Deepak Chopra, Bob Proctor, Anthony Robbins, The Secret, and others over the years, along with yoga, meditation, Vipassana – etc. They all certainly helped me in my personal growth.

I am glad I studied and meditated, and I am still a student of learning in this world. I will be, till the day I leave for the next world!

TAROT gave me the instant answers to my questions every-step-of-the-way … AND FAST and FURIOUS.

But we must listen to the subtle nuances of the cards and overcome EGO. Replace it with INTUITION. The quicker you can do this, the quicker you will see your life evolve like magic!

Introduction Day 1

Create Your FUTURE

THE FUTURE

Remember your future does not just happen, unless you let it happen TO you and not FOR you

Tarot is for Everyone including YOU!

One day, I realized I had created my life over the last thirty years with my trust in the Tarot for guidance.

I started reading for others, obtained my professional certification as A Tarot Reader and Advisor (Tarot Guild of Australia) and found people from around the globe were giving me feedback that I had changed their lives.

Not by predicting their future as other Tarot readers may do but by showing them how to create their future lives with the Tarot as their guide.

When I got their personalities and past and present energies right – or amazingly spot on as they said, they were then very accepting that I could show them how to create their future with the guidance of the Tarot Cards.

Remember your future does not just happen, unless you let it happen TO you and not FOR you. I now have a keen desire to help like-minded and **purpose-driven people who are ready to reach their full potential in their lives as I have done.** You do not have to be a fifth-generation psychic or talk to dead people to benefit. Tarot is for EVERYONE – including you!

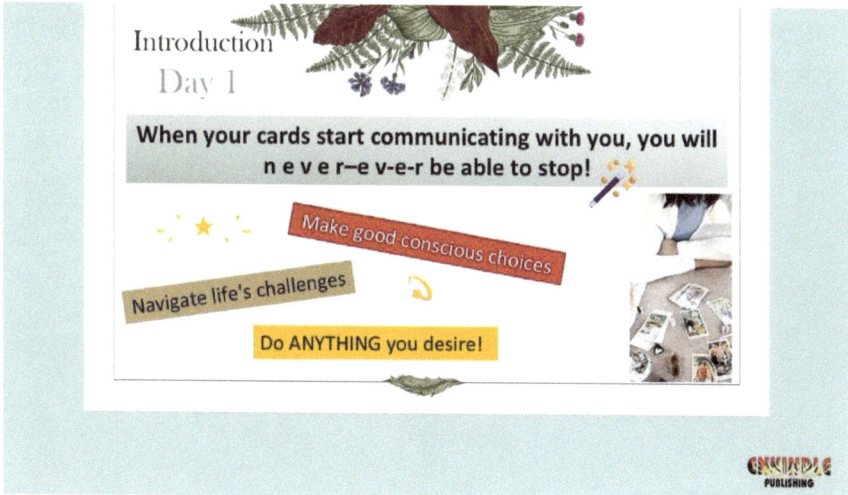

Introduction
Day 1

When your cards start communicating with you, you will n e v e r—e v-e-r be able to stop!

Make good conscious choices

Navigate life's challenges

Do ANYTHING you desire!

By consulting the Tarot cards, you can empower yourself to navigate life's challenges, make good conscious choices, be successful in your career, create a business, and attract the love of your life ... the list goes on and is never-ending. You can do ANYTHING you desire! **Believe me – because I did.**

- business owner of training colleges
- award winning author of children's illustrated books and non-fiction romance
- screenwriter
- professional Tarot advisor
- counsellor
- artist

Not least of all, I met my true-life partner at the age of seventeen, married him at twenty-three and we have been together a lifetime.

I bet as you start to work with your Tarot cards, and they start communicating with you, you will n e v e r—e v-e-r be able to stop!

You don't have to learn traditional spreads. Well, you can certainly delve into that later if you wish. There are many teachings on the subject. This way – my way will get you going right now!

Don't be impatient. Absorb. Understand. Read the Cards.

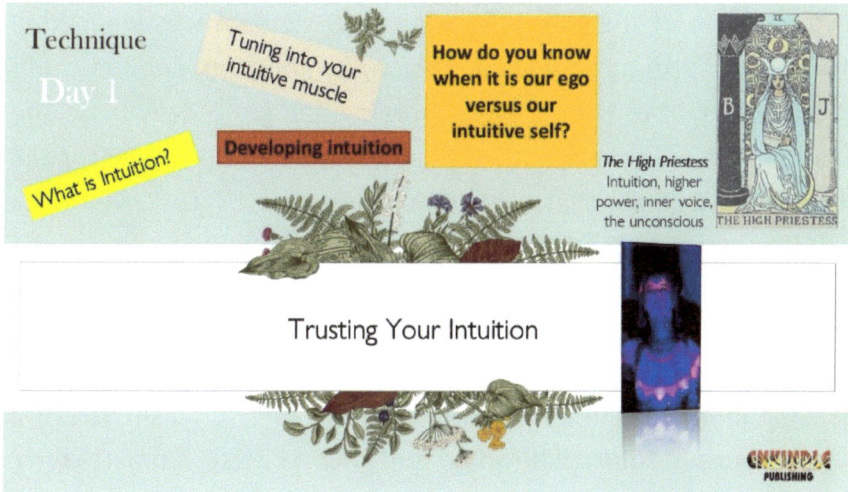

Technique
Day 1
What is Intuition?
Tuning into your intuitive muscle
Developing intuition
How do you know when it is our ego versus our intuitive self?

The High Priestess
Intuition, higher power, inner voice, the unconscious

THE HIGH PRIESTESS

Trusting Your Intuition

ENKINDLE
PUBLISHING

I am going to unpack

- What is intuition?
- How do you know when it is our ego versus our intuitive self?
- Developing intuition and tuning into your intuitive muscle.

Reading Tarot successfully is all about trusting in your intuition. Once you have connected with your intuition during a Tarot reading, that is when the magic starts to happen. But until you reach that place, you have self-doubt. How do I trust my intuition? Is it my intuition talking or is it something else?

This happened to me and is quite normal. Particularly in my case, it was extremely hard to learn to trust in my intuition.

I come from a background where I was sent to boarding school – a convent boarding school where I stayed from the age of 7 to 17, visiting home maybe 5 times over those formative years on brief visits over the Christmas holidays. My mother was a devout Catholic – my father not so, but he pretended to be, to avoid the wrath of his wife and dutifully accompanied her to church every Sunday.

In those days of the late 1950's the Catholic faith was steeped in rituals. Rituals of attending confession, communion, and mass. For us kids, we had to get up every morning and go to daily mass and were told the Devil would get us and we would go to hell for the slightest mischief that young children get into. We were indoctrinated into the faith as it was then.

When I grew up and left school and went to work in the big city I completely turned into an "atheist" as my mother labelled me. I became interested in Buddhist philosophy and Hinduism amongst other strains of spiritual development such as Reiki, Aromatherapy, Crystal Healing, and later Tarot. At that time, Tarot was very much looked upon as the Devil's work by some and thought of merely as fortune-telling by most.

When Tarot worked for me as my friend and guide, that is when I got hooked! I began genuinely believing it when I consulted the Tarot and took the guidance of the cards that appeared, things started working out magically! From that new hunk, I attracted – well he looked like Elvis of whom I was a great fan and still am BTW, to helping me get that extra work to pay the rent that month.

But there is a secret to reading the Tarot RIGHT.

It is simple.

Don't fear. Just promise me to listen … and A-B-S-O-R-B.

Intuition is our ability to know something without reasoning

We know what is about to happen

★+⁺•⋅)○(⋅•⁺⋅★

Intuition is the thing of knowing something without really knowing why you know it

ENKINDLE
PUBLISHING

Day 1

Intuition is our ability to know something without reasoning.

It's not all about connecting with your Spirit Guides or Angels or woo-woo stuff. If that is the way you connect with your intuition – that is impressive, but it does not have to be.

It is when we feel as if we know **what is about to happen or what to do without** having any real facts.

Fact: I was waiting for a lift in India with my father after his business meeting in a high-rise building on the 32nd floor. We were to go to lunch at the restaurant on the ground floor. I had come up in that same lift to meet him. But as the lift arrived and everyone crowded in as they tend to do in India – I held back with my hand on his arm.

"We will wait for the next one Dad" I said.

"There's a place Ma'am – come," said a polite young Indian man.

I shook my head. "Thanks – no," I said.

All the auras surrounding those people turned black. That lift crashed to the floor and all twenty-six people died.

I learnt about intuition at the age of nineteen.

Intuition is the thing of knowing something without really knowing why you know it.

Technique

There is a DIFFERENCE between
INSTINCT ⇔ INTUITION

Instinct is an inborn tendency

Instinct is our natural reaction

The Right Brain is our creative side

The Magician
Being resourceful,
ability, skill,
manifestation,
creativity

Day 1

ENKINDLE
PUBLISHING

Instinct is different from intuition. It is an inborn tendency.

Instinct is our natural reaction; it occurs without even thinking. If someone is lying on the road in a car accident you just witnessed, you rush to help as best as you can. Call 911 for help and comfort the victim.

Fact: I saw a man drop from a heart attack once in a shopping centre. The instinct was CPR immediately. I had not learnt CPR at that time, just watched what they do on Grey's Anatomy! TV shows have their use sometimes!

When we are in rational thought, we work out things methodically and plan, but in our intuitive mindset, it all happens on that unseen, unknowing level.

It is something you feel more in the heart or the stomach – that gut feeling. The heart space is that connection with pure love and pure energy. If we work from that space, we will connect with our intuition perfectly.

It is the pure essence of who we are, that helps us understand things in ways that we do not understand why we understand it. Right?!

The Left Brain is our more logical and rational side. The Right Brain is our creative side. Intuition is associated with the Right Brain. The Right Brain thrives on creativity – visualization, imagery, beauty symbolism. It is more of a feeling/sensing place.

All those things are important when you want to start to create and connect with your intuition.

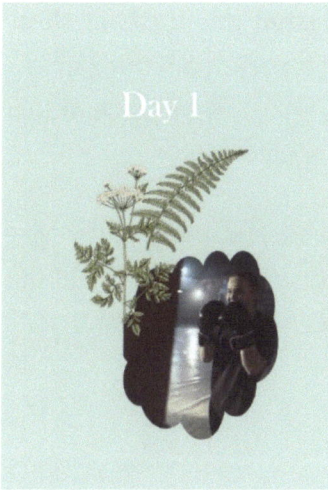

Technique

How do you know when it is our

Ego

Versus

our **Intuitive Self?**

Seven of Cups
choices, illusion,
wishful thinking,
indecision

Firstly, know that Ego operates from a place of Fear.

When we connect and tune in from a place of **love, we can let go of all** attachment to a particular outcome because we are operating from the heart. Pure love energy. We are then much more open and receptive to **what our intuition wants to tell us.**

Fear tends to express itself in terms of scarcity or lack, or thinking of the reasons why we shouldn't have what we are asking for at the same time we draw the cards and lay them out seeking our answer. We worry that we are not going to have enough of something or are negating the question subconsciously.

For example – your question to the Tarot may be:

"Will I meet my future husband this year?"

But in your subconscious, you are saying "No, I don't want to be tied to a long-term partnership as yet. I want to travel and advance my career, but I wonder what the cards will say hmm …"

Please know, because I have tried and tested this for over thirty years in my life – remember I told you I don't teach anything unless it works for me – ask yourself "Am I connecting from a place of fear or subconscious negation, or is this really what I want?"

The Tarot will always tell you what you need to know to get where you want to get. In this scenario, you may get messages about travel and career opportunities. You will then think "I can't read the Tarot" and give up.

Wrong. You have read the cards very well.

Just not got the answer you wanted.

Intuition also shows up in our lives in the way it keeps presenting us with the same lesson over and over.

If we are working with ego, we ignore it, don't want to listen to it and things start happening.

For example: Maybe you don't take enough care of yourself. You're a workaholic and don't eat healthy meals. You get a cold. And then if you don't pay attention, you get worse with pneumonia and end up in hospital – hope not! This is not because you have bad health. You have not paid attention to your intuition and the message of the UNIVERSE!

It may manifest itself in different ways, but it will keep showing up until you pay attention to it.

Day 1

Technique

Developing intuition
Tuning into your intuitive muscle

Serendipity

Intuitive Muscle

Tune in

Confidence

ENKINDLE
PUBLISHING

Your intuition shows up in very persistent and loud ways. It is important to check in on what you are thinking: Is it a place of lack or is it a place of abundance? Is it a place of fear or is it a place of love? Is it a place of really what I want and not ego?

You learn better from doing it, experiencing it, and progressing as you go. I have always been one to do something before worrying that I need to wait to learn it all or pass exams – put the cart before the horse as it were.

Yes, it does work, believe me, after thirty years of my way, you are going to learn to do it too! It is not a big secret – just needs common sense and confidence.

People say to me – "you have a gift. Amazing intuition."

I think everybody is intuitive. But we choose whether we are going to listen to that intuition and overcome the ego.

When you tune in to your radio, sometimes you get a buzzing sound, sometimes a broken sentence by the newsreader, and sometimes a song repeats itself.

Just like your intuition. You are not tuned in.

Maybe like the radio and the different frequencies, you are kind of in between radio frequencies. The more you work on it and turn the dial into your intuition until you get a clear signal, you will develop your intuition.

No fear. No negating your question subconsciously. Just trusting the Universe to deliver your abundance with NO LIMITS.

It does take work.

You cannot have something without putting in the effort. Believe me, build your intuitive muscle. Take it to the gym of meditation, yoga, or any other spiritual practice you like. I don't go to the gym and lift weights or run on the treadmill. I am into yoga, and Vipassana meditation.

Whatever floats your boat. Healthy body – healthy mind.

Eat well and exercise your intuitive muscle. The more you work with your intuition, the more it will grow in your life.

If you desire Tarot to guide you to a successful, happy life in love, career and everyday ebb and flow, please work on this one skill. It is the secret to reading Tarot successfully for yourself.

It is not just about how you do Tarot either, but how you lead your life from an intuitive place where serendipity takes place and things start to flow.

Listen

Change

Apply

The Process

ENKINDLE
PUBLISHING

My Process is easy to follow just come with me on this journey ...

I really want you to succeed in CREATING WHAT YOU DESIRE! The Tarot is the best friend you can have, if you are prepared to do the work. Remember I said YOU need to Listen, Change, and Apply the new Techniques.

Yes of course you can do it! All that is required is a willingness on your part. It is just commonsense.

The Journeyer

READY?! WELL, LET'S GET STARTED!

Let's get into it to read Tarot for yourself and create your life! We are going to read Tarot from the Heart *not* the Book.

Why?

It is my successful, tried, and tested way and I'm teaching you to read Tarot to enhance your life. You can go on to read for others if you wish. In this mini course, I am adamant I am going to teach like-minded people to achieve their goals in their lives. Here are the 78 cards of the Tarot. **I would like you to look at the pictures.** Spend some time looking at each of them, as we begin to call on the magic of the Tarot for each of you!

Eventually, they will talk to you, and you will see things in the cards from your visual intuitive mind.

To begin with, I will explain, and we will follow the general meanings of each card briefly till this happens. And it will, I promise you! **For some, it is sooner than later.** But for everyone, it will happen. Remember not to NEGATE your first impressions and feelings as you look at a card.

Why should you not memorize each card? It doesn't work. What is happening is that you're using your critical mind for the reading. Your intuitive mind is not working. In doing so it's shutting down your intuition.

When you are memorizing, you are in the logical, critical thinking mode and it is shutting out your intuition. Which believe you me is always right. Don't knock it!

I don't know about you, but I want intuitive readings, not by the book. You can get computer generated readings for that. The app for "Yes and No" answers for instance is random and will generate a "Yes" answer and then a "Maybe" or a "No" answer at random.

The computer doesn't have intuition. Even with today's AI intelligence, it is still a robot. Clever but not intuitive as your human brain.

So, familiarize yourself with the 78 Tarot Cards. Look at them. Then put them aside. Don't try to memorize them. For now, just remember there are 21 Major Arcana and 4 Suits totalling 56 cards. Now if you're good at Maths, that is 77 cards. Who is the 78th card? He is the Fool. The Fool is the Journeyer numbered at 0. He makes his journey though each of the cards, meeting new teachers and learning new life lessons along the way. Eventually he reaches the completion of his journey with the World card.

As we follow the Fool's journey, we can see parallels between our own life stages and those in the cards. Each card teaches a specific lesson and concept to meditate upon.

I will explain as we go along.

THE JOURNEYER

Major Arcana ✨

THE MAGICIAN.   THE HIGH PRIESTESS   THE EMPRESS.   THE EMPEROR.

Major Arcana

Major Arcana

THE HERMIT.   WHEEL of FORTUNE.   JUSTICE.   THE HANGED MAN.   DEATH.   TEMPERANCE.   THE DEVIL.

Major Arcana

Suit of Wands

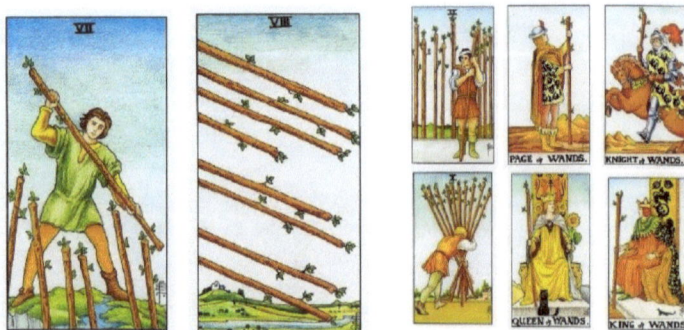

Suit of Wands

Suit of Cups

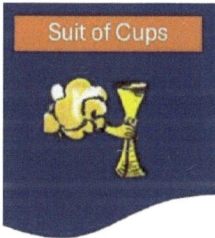

Suit of Swords

Suit of Pentacles

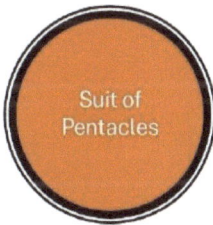

Suit of
Pentacles

The Major Arcana cards are a very powerful source of spiritual wisdom and insight.

The Major Arcana deals with life events and is referred to as The Fool's Journey. The Fool is the main character of the Major Arcana and makes his journey through each of the cards. They represent life lessons, karmic influence and the big archetypal themes that influence each of our individual life journeys.

Spiritual evolution occurs in the Three Stages of the Major Arcana: Conscious, Unconscious, and Superconscious.

The **Conscious stage** starts at the Magician and ends with the Chariot. In this stage, we are learning how the world works. The lessons we learn often come from our parents, caregivers and immediate community. This is our early conditioning. The societal rules and ideology of the world that we were born into. This stage is our youth.

The **Unconscious stage** begins at Strength and ends in Temperance. In this stage we've learned about how the world works, and how to fulfill our basic needs, we begin to think about what else there can be. We face challenges and moral quandaries which give us the opportunity to grow. We must deal with our fears and desires. In this stage we are provided with the lessons that we must learn to grow and evolve and forge a sense of identity. This stage is our adulthood.

The **Superconscious** stage starts at the Devil and ends at the World. In this stage we are connecting to a higher power to help us find our spiritual purpose. We have developed a clear sense of self and are searching for purpose and possibly an awakening. We are looking for a sense of oneness with the Universe and all living things. This stage is often associated with the wisdom that comes with age.

However, we do not have to be of biological old age to reach this stage. Have you ever heard of people saying he or she is an old soul? We can have reached this stage earlier in our lives. We can miss some early lessons, only to learn them later. Some of us find some lessons difficult to learn and are forced to repeat them over and over again until we finally absorb their wisdom.

The Fool's journey is an archetype. In real life, our lives are variations of this. These stages are a guideline, but there is no one size that fits all. We take different paths.

What lessons have you learned and have yet to learn? What lessons have been particularly difficult for you to accept?

Each of you are here to learn how to create your future.

Learning from past experiences is important because it helps us make better decisions and avoid repeating the same mistakes. By reflecting on our past successes and failures, we can gain valuable insights into what worked well and what didn't and use that information to guide our future actions.

Learning the lessons of the past is the only way to shape the present and the future.

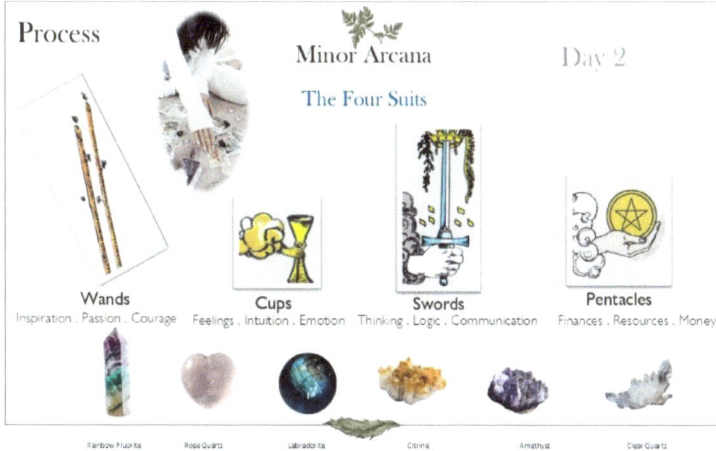

Process   Minor Arcana   Day 2

The Four Suits

Wands	Cups	Swords	Pentacles
Inspiration . Passion . Courage	Feelings . Intuition . Emotion	Thinking . Logic . Communication	Finances . Resources . Money

Rainbow Fluorite   Rose Quartz   Labradorite   Citrine   Amethyst   Clear Quartz

The Minor Arcana deal with the everyday side of things. The flux and flow of life is represented in the Minor Arcana. The Minor Arcana will tell us what we are experiencing on a day-to-day basis and the situations we get ourselves into.

The Minor Arcana will tell us what is happening, whereas the Major Arcana will tell us why it is happening. It is through the Minor Arcana the Major Arcana expresses itself. Whatever the Major Arcana wish to express becomes manifest in The Minor Arcana.

The Minor Arcana effectively bring to life the abstract world of the Major as it plays out its driving energy in how we think, act, feel and behave on a day-to-day basis.

- **Pentacles** – money, material things, health, finances, work

- **Swords** – intellect, power, knowledge, change

- **Cups** – emotions, love, feelings, intuition, relationships

41

- **Wands** – Inspiration, new passion, enthusiasm, energy, determination, strength, intuition, creativity, ambition, and expansion

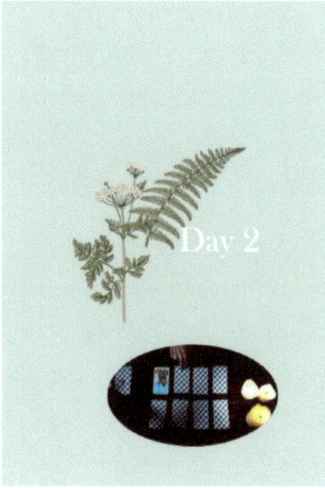

Process

Swords	Ace-2-3-4-5-6-7-8-9-10. Page. Knight. Queen. King
Cups	Ace-2-3-4-5-6-7-8-9-10. Page. Knight. Queen. King
Wands	Ace-2-3-4-5-6-7-8-9-10. Page. Knight. Queen. King
Pentacles	Ace-2-3-4-5-6-7-8-9-10. Page. Knight. Queen. King

In All Suits

- Page can be youth or children.
- Knight is the symbol of youth between the ages of 18 & 30.
- Queen and King are females or males who are mature or married.

EXAMPLE Suit of Cups

This is a mini course and a course to get you to understand the Tarot quickly and to read for guidance in your own life.

I am making it as simple as possible. I want you to commence getting guidance in your life. I want you to start developing your Intuition.

So here we go – remember I said just remember there are 21 Major Arcana + The Fool, and the four Suits of the Minor Arcana 56 cards:

Each of the Suits is numbered one to ten.

The Ace in each Suit is always No.1. similar to playing cards if you are familiar with card games!

Then we have the Court Cards in each Suit following No. 10. Page. Knight. Queen. King. They are not numbered.

- Swords Ace-2-3-4-5-6-7-8-9-10. Page. Knight. Queen. King

- Cups Ace-2-3-4-5-6-7-8-9-10. Page. Knight. Queen. King

- Wands Ace-2-3-4-5-6-7-8-9-10. Page. Knight. Queen. King

- Pentacles Ace-2-3-4-5-6-7-8-9-10. Page.

- Knight. Queen. King

Repeating here -

Page can be youth or children. Knight is the symbol of youth between the ages of 18 & 30. Queen and King are females or males who are mature or married. As a *person* in your life their personalities can be determined by their Suit.

A *message or situation* can also be determined by their Suit.

Example: **Cups** is about feelings, emotions, and creativity.

Page of Cups

Personality traits are on emotion and opening those emotions to allow compassion and love for others. As a situation or message, it represents an opportunity for artistic or creative learning and expansion. New opportunities for relationships.

Knight of Cups

Personality traits are kind and caring and in touch with intuition and emotions. Compassion and understanding towards others because they have learned to understand their own feelings and emotions.

As a situation or message, you are making decisions based on how you feel about a situation rather than what you think, even if others can't make sense of what you are doing and why, and your intuition guides you in everything you do.

Queen of Cups

Personality traits are nurturing, caring, compassionate, empathic, and sensitive. They don't take on other people's energy or emotional issues because they are well-grounded and know where to create a healthy separation.

As a situation or message others come to them to confide their personal issues regarding relationships, emotions, and feelings. They help others as a counsellor, healer or just a good friend.

King of Cups

Personality traits are emotionally balanced, compassionate, diplomatic.

As a situation or message, you can draw on your emotional maturity and stability to help you navigate challenges, even when life throws you a curve ball. You don't let things get to you and you steer clear of drama, choosing an emotionally balanced and calm approach.

Process

The 78 Tarot Cards

The Major Arcana	The Four Suits	The Court Cards
21 Cards	Numbered 1 to 10	Page . Knight . Queen . King
The Three Realms	40 cards	16 cards
The Conscious Realm	The Suit of Wands	The Court of Wands
Unconscious Realm	The Suit of Cups	The Court of Cups
The Superconscious Realm	The Suit of Swords	The Court of Swords
	The Suit of Pentacles	The Court of Pentacles

Day 2

The Tarot Cards

The Journeyer THE FOOL

ENKINDLE
PUBLISHING

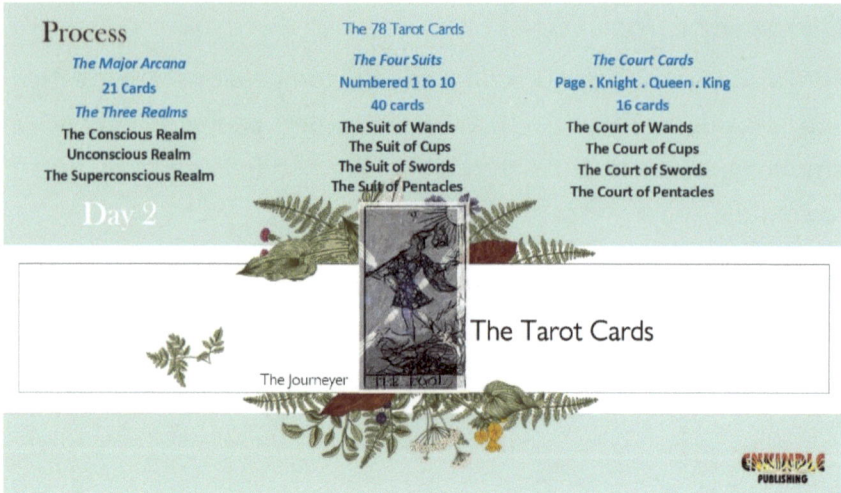

Ok, so revising what we have learnt There are:

78 cards of the Tarot divided into Major Arcana and Minor Arcana.

21 **Major Arcana + the Fool** numbered at 0. The Major Arcana are divided into the 3 realms,

Unconscious – learning how the world works.

Subconscious – our inward search to find out who we really are.

Superconscious – development of spiritual awareness and a sense of self.

The Fool is the Journeyer embarking on The Fool's journey through the Major Arcana meeting his teachers and experiencing the lessons of the flux and flow of life through the 4 suits of the Minor Arcana along his way.

4 Suits of the Minor Arcana consist of 56 cards each suit having 14 cards.

- **Pentacles** – money, material things, health, finances, work

- **Swords** – intellect, power, knowledge, change

- **Cups** – emotions, love, feelings, intuition, relationships

- **Wands** - Inspiration, new passion, enthusiasm, energy, determination, strength, intuition, creativity, ambition, and expansion

The Court cards of the Minor Arcana are Page, Knight, Queen and King. They can represent people or situations and events.

Trust your INTUITION

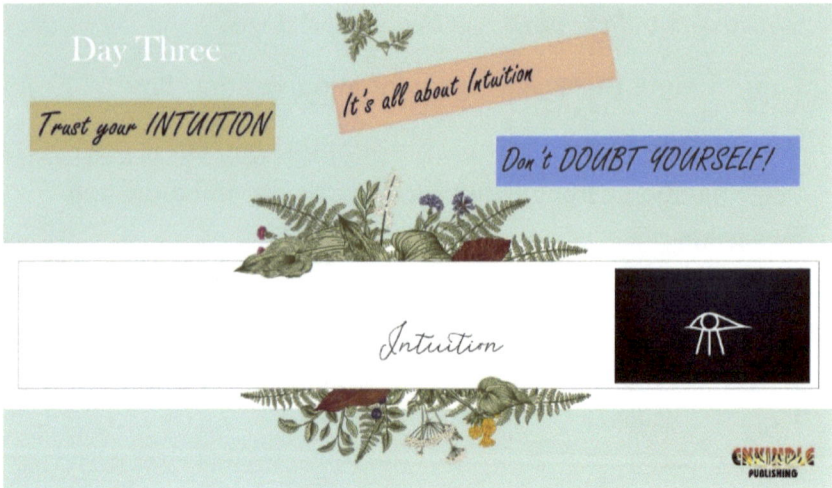

It's all about Intuition

Don't DOUBT YOURSELF!

Intuition

CHRONICLE
PUBLISHING

It's all about Intiution!

Intuition is the most important part of working with the Tarot as your friend. Let's ask your Tarot cards to be your friend!

Remember we talked about intuition in the beginning. To refresh your memory – Intuition is something that we know, without knowing why we know it!

Trust your INTUITION, the TAROT and your ancestors and guides that want to help you.

This mini course is all about developing your intuition.

The Tarot is the tool that helps you do this in a BIG WAY!

Also Simple, Easy, and Quick.

You don't have to attend a great number of seminars and courses on personal growth, just follow the advice of the Tarot and develop your OWN intuition.

Everything we need to know is WITHIN US. We just need to tap into the KNOWING!

DON'T DOUBT yourself!

Remember, when working with your Spirit Self and guides **there are no mistakes.**

Stay true to your initial interpretation. Trust.

Start using your INTUITION
Worksheet

Past

Present

Guidance for YOUR Future

Guidance Chart

I look at the individual's past and the present in relation to their question. This will give a true picture of where they are heading in the future.

Are the lessons of the past being ignored in the present? These would need to be addressed before they can get what they desire that comes up in their future. These are future possibilities. Not set in stone. Achievable, but will not come to pass, unless ACTION IS TAKEN!

My belief after thirty years of experiencing this, is that Tarot does predict your future, but only you have the power and free will to *create* your future and get what you want in life – that dream job, the true love of your life or good health and peace of mind.

Also please remember, that you can always co-create or re-create with the Universe, you have free will and the Universe always has your back. I did. It has worked for me.

Here I am teaching you to create your own life and what you desire in YOUR FUTURE.

So, let's go. You have a head-start. You know your past. You know what it happening in your present.

But do you know what you are repeating now from your past? If things are recurring now which you wish were not happening – then yes you are repeating the lessons not learnt from the past and are not aware of it.

So, we are going to look at your past first and your present as well – before we draw any card for the future. Don't be impatient.

Do you notice that Tarot readers just draw your cards for the future when you ask – Will I meet my true-life partner soon? You will get a "right" answer and that perfect person does come into your life as predicted. You get all excited and say "Wow" wasn't that reader so on point – so correct. Yes, the reader was correct at the time. Then it doesn't last, and the relationship goes south.

WHY?

Hey! You need to attract that person when you are in the right energy, or you will most probably end up with the same broken relationship as in your past? Has it happened once, twice or more before in your life?

Fact:
I was asked the other day by a man who wanted to know if he would reconcile with his wife.

He said she had treated him horrifically (his words) and he was going to divorce her. He also said his wife wanted him to disappear from her life and told him that the last six years of her life had been wasted with him. They had a child of about a year-old together.

BUT he loved her and felt she was his one and only and his soulmate and true-life partner.

As we delved into his past (six relationships) they seem to have ended one way or another for which he blamed the other person, the woman.

Looking at his past and personality, he now understands he needs to work on himself to attract the right relationship, whether it will be a reconciliation with his wife or not.

Then I drew the Four of Wands for him in his future– a genuine lasting love and happy home life! A prediction of his Future which gives him hope. But it won't just happen. It must be created. The work needs to be done. Action taken.

I have written the intuitive Tarot Guide with my personal intuitive thoughts to guide you. Refer to it. However, I will stress, please refer to it only when you first start. Let your intuition take over – don't kill it by trying to memorize. Repeat don't memorize – just refer and let your intuition take over. You are going to start seeing your own intuitive messages in the cards pertaining to the question you ask of the Tarot.

Have a look at an example of a Tarot reading first to get an idea of how to go about your reading.

Intuitive Guide of the 78 Tarot Cards

No.0 THE FOOL

Beginnings, youth, spontaneity, a free spirit
The Journeyer. The archetype through life's journey.
Similarities in our navigation through life's journey
Comes to mind -
- a happy dog
- packed with very little baggage
- ready for adventure
- prepared to take risks?

What do YOU see? What does it mean to you?

No.1 THE MAGICIAN

Manifestation, resourcefulness, willpower, ability
New Beginnings and Opportunities
Comes to mind –
- the four symbols of the Tarot. He can create the reality he desires with the tools he is given
- infinity symbol gives him unlimited potential
- flowers blooming – his ideas are coming to fruition

What do YOU see? What does it mean to you?

No.2 THE HIGH PRIESTESS

Intuition, higher power, inner voice, self-trust, wisdom
Allow intuition to flourish. Trust what your intuition has to say
Comes to mind –
- black and white pillars of duality masculine and feminine
- a scroll ready to unfold with knowledge beyond the material realm
- crescent moon a symbol of connection to the divine feminine and cycles of the moon

What do YOU see? What does it mean to you?

No.3 THE EMPRESS
sensuality, fertility, nurturing, creativity, beauty, abundance
Bring abundance to yourself and everyone under your care
Comes to mind -
- a lush forest, stream, connection to Mother Nature
- golden wheat ready to harvest which is abundance
- pomegranates are fertility
- symbol of Venus, which is love, fertility, beauty and grace

What do YOU see? What does it mean to you?

No.4 THE EMPEROR
Authority, protection, stability, practicality, focus, discipline
Practice your personal power while maintaining boundaries
Comes to mind -
- an Ankh the Egyptian symbol of life and an Orb the symbol of the world he rules
- long white beard which shows wisdom and golden crown which demands he is heard
- a mountain range. He is immovable unless he deems it necessary to change his views

What do YOU see? What does it mean to you?

No.5 THE HIEROPHANT
Tradition, conventionality, conformity, education, beliefs, knowledge
I can find belonging with people who accept me as I am
Comes to mind -
- crossed keys the symbol of balance between the conscious and unconscious minds which only he can teach
- religious beliefs as signified with the Papal scepter
- three-tiered crown signifying the three realms over which he rules
- two followers kneel before him which represent a group identity and the rite of passage to enter in the next level

What do YOU see? What does it mean to you?

No.6 THE LOVERS

Love, partnerships, relationships, romance, choices
Love reveals itself through my everyday actions
Comes to mind -

- serpent and apple tree, garden of Eden depicting sensual pleasures
- angel Raphael showing the couple the path from physical desire to emotional needs to spiritual concerns
- volcanic mountain looks phallic like the eruption of passion between man and woman

What do YOU see? What does it mean to you?

No.7 THE CHARIOT

Success, ambition, victory, control, willpower
I know when to exert determination and when to let go
Comes to mind -

- laurel wreath and star crown show victory
- not holding reins using strength of will and mind to drive
- stands tall not sitting down. He is about acting and moving forward
- sphinxes pull in opposite directions. He uses willpower to steer them forward in the direction he wants

What do YOU see? What does it mean to you?

No.8 STRENGTH

Courage, bravery, confidence ,inner power, compassion
I acknowledge my animal instincts which are part of me but not all of me
Comes to mind –

- lion depicts raw passion and desires
- woman holds the jaw and calms lion. Can I control my instincts?
- white robe with flowers showing purity of spirit and expression of nature
- infinity symbol showing infinite potential and wisdom

What do YOU see? What does it mean to you?

55

No.9 THE HERMIT
Self-reflection, introspection, contemplation, solitude, search for self
In silence and solitude, I can allow my inner voice to speak to guide me to my soul, my self
Comes to mind –
- lantern to light the way to next steps
- a staff to guide and balance
- light with 6-point star denotes wisdom
What do YOU see? What does it mean to you?

No.10 WHEEL OF FORTUNE
Change, life cycles, fate, unexpected events, luck, fortune, decisive moment, karma, turning point
Circumstances change, but I remain calm and centered
Comes to mind –
- a snake depicting the material force descending into the world
- sphinx (wisdom of gods and kings) and Anubis (underworld) top and bottom rotate with the wheel as it goes up and down
- an angel, bull, eagle and lion with wings depicting the four evangelists in Christian tradition
What do YOU see? What does it mean to you?

No.11 JUSTICE
Justice, karma, accountability, truth, honesty, integrity, cause and effect
In silence and solitude, I can allow my inner voice to speak to guide me to my soul, my self
Comes to mind –
- scales represent balance
- double-edged sword represents impartiality
- white shoe peeping out, reminds us that our actions always carry consequences
What do YOU see? What does it mean to you?

56

No.12 THE HANGED MAN

Waiting, uncertainty, lack of direction, sacrifice
Life doesn't always flow in forward motion. Some awakenings cannot be forced, but I can be open to them when the time comes
Comes to mind –
- hanging by one foot to the tree of life, other foot is free
- face is serene. It is his own choice
- halo round his head symbolizing new insight, awareness and enlightenment
What do YOU see? What does it mean to you?

No.13 DEATH

Transformation, change, endings, letting go, release
Loss can open the door to new beginnings. All endings are also new beginnings
Comes to mind –
- corpses define we are all the same in death whether paupers or kings
- white horse is purity. Death purifies everything it touches
- scythe depicts no bargaining can save us from the scythe. We will all die in our time.
What do YOU see? What does it mean to you?

No.14 TEMPERANCE

Balance, peace, patience, moderation, harmony, serenity, finding a middle way
I am not one thing or another. I can blend multiple perspectives to create who I am
Comes to mind –
- two cups mixing waters defining the mixing of unconscious and conscious minds
- one foot in water and one foot on dry land also representing the unconscious and conscious
- an androgynous angel, suggesting the balance of masculine and feminine energies
What do YOU see? What does it mean to you?

No.15 THE DEVIL

Obsession, addiction, dependency, excess, limitations
Knowing my weaknesses helps me become a better person.
The Devil signifies our shadow self who holds the spirit in
bondage
Comes to mind –
- a man and a woman held captive chained
- horns on the man and woman as if it signifies that
  the more time they spend with the Devil, the less
  human they become
What do YOU see? What does it mean to you?

No.16 THE TOWER

Breakthrough, wake-up call, sudden change, upheaval, chaos
I have courage to break the structures that need to be broken in
my life. Destruction cleanses and clears the way for a better life
Comes to mind –
- high tower built on crumbling foundation represents
  ambitions and goals built on false foundations
- lightning strikes representing sudden insight into a
  revelation or a breakthrough
- flames alight the tower forcing people to jump out of the
  tower not knowing what awaits them when they fall
What do YOU see? What does it mean to you?

No.17 THE STAR

Hope, inspiration, positivity, faith, renewal, healing, hope
When all is lost, hope still shines like a guiding star. I will trust that
the Universe will provide for me
Comes to mind –
- two containers of water represent the conscious and
  unconscious. She pours the water to nourish the earth and
  continue the cycle of fertility
- she is naked symbolizing her purity under the sky
- large star representing her core essence with seven stars
  representing the 7 chakras
What do YOU see? What does it mean to you?

No.18 THE MOON

Illusion, uncertainty, secrets, anxiety, fears

When everything without reflects what is within, I will not be fearful and will be my own light. I learn to differentiate between illusion and intuition

Comes to mind –

- a wolf and a dog representing the two sides of our nature, tame and wild
- two towers similar in appearance represent good and evil and the difficulty we face in distinguishing between them
- the moon is dim only slightly illuminating the path to consciousness compared to the sun

What do YOU see? What does it mean to you?

No.19 THE SUN

Happiness, success, truth, vitality, joy, confidence

I illuminate what needs to see the light. I let my light shine through to others

Comes to mind –

- a naked child sitting on top of a calm white horse. The child representing innocence and purity and the horse representing purity and strength
- the sunflower turns its face to the light of the sun, so too does the face of humanity turn to the light of Truth

What do YOU see? What does it mean to you?

No.20 JUDGEMENT

Self-evaluation, awakening, renewal, purpose ,a change of heart

I act in alignment with my purpose and principles

Comes to mind –

- naked men women and children rise from their graves symbolizing that they are ready to be judged by the Universe and their creator
- the massive tidal wave signifies the washing away of the world and that the ruling will be final
- angel Gabriel the Messenger of God blowing his trumpet, calls them to judgement

What do YOU see? What does it mean to you?

No.21 THE WORLD
Completion, achievement, fulfillment, sense of belonging
I am shaped and molded by the Universe. I now encounter a greater consciousness and live in harmony with it
Comes to mind –
- naked woman stepping through a circular laurel wreath looking back at the past moving on to the next phase in a continuous cycle
- two wands or baton symbols like the Magician holds symbolizes that what was manifested with the Magician has now come to completion with the World

What do YOU see? What does it mean to you?

CUPS Intuitive Emotional Suit 🌑 💟 💝 💘 represents feelings and can refer to people and relationships and how you react to others and the environment

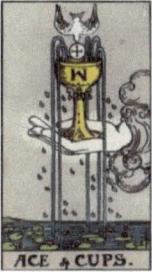

Love, new feelings, awakening emotions	Unity, attraction, partnership	Friendship, gatherings, celebration	Indifference, discontent, boredom	Loss, sadness, disappointment
Nostalgia, memories, familiarity	Illusion, wishful thinking, indecision	Moving on, walking away, abandonment	Satisfaction, success, wishes coming true	Happiness, fulfillment, domestic harmony

PAGE of CUPS.	KNIGHT of CUPS.	QUEEN of CUPS.	KING of CUPS.
Idealism, sensitivity, A dreamer	Charming, artistic, idealist	Compassionate, healer, counsellor	Wisdom, diplomacy, an advisor

PENTACLES Physical and Material Suit 🧍 🪙 💼 🍀 deals with health, finances and work. What we make of our outer surroundings – how we create it, shape it, transform it and grow it.

ACE of PENTACLES	II	III	IV	
New opportunities, abundance, prosperity	Balancing resources, adaption, flexibility	Teamwork, effort, collaboration	Possessiveness, insecurity, guardedness	Hardship, loss, isolation

Material help, sharing, gratitude	Diligence, evaluation, progress	Skill, commitment, dedication	Independence, self-sufficiency, rewarded efforts	Tradition, foundations, family
A planner, being goal oriented, consistency	Practicality, slow and steady, reliability	Good business sense, homebody, generosity	Businessman, abundance, prosperity	

SWORDS Mind and Intellect Suit 💭 😰 💀 💡 deals with thinking and logic. Swords mirror the quality of mind present in your thoughts, attitudes, and beliefs. The double edge of the sword symbolises the fine balance between intellect and power

Clarity, vision, truth	Difficult choices, denial, stuck in the middle	Heartbreak, sadness, trauma	Recuperation, rest, sanctuary	Arguments, stress, intimidation

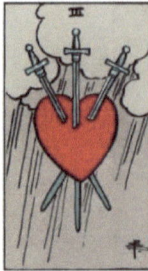

Moving on, departure, accepting lessons	Indecision, betrayal, deception	Feeling trapped, helplessness, restriction	Fear, anxiety, breaking point	Bitterness, betrayal, victimization

PAGE of SWORDS.
Curiosity, wit, mental agility,

KNIGHT of SWORDS.
An intellectual, assertiveness, directness

QUEEN of SWORDS.
Constructive criticism, fairness, honesty

KING of SWORDS.
High standards, discipline, integrity

WANDS Original Thought and the Seeds through which Life springs forth Suit 🌱 ✴️ 💪 😇 🎯 Wands deals with primal energy, spirituality, inspiration, determination, strength, intuition, creativity, ambition and expansion

ACE of WANDS.
Intuition, new initiative, expansion

II
Planning, first steps, taking risks

III
Expansion, growth, foresight

IV
Home, celebrations, reunions

V
Clashes of ego, competition, conflict

Success, praise, recognition	Standing up for self, protectiveness, self-belief	Movement, sudden changes, quick decisions	Fatigue, taking a last stand, close to success	Burden, struggles responsibility,

PAGE of WANDS. — **KNIGHT of WANDS.** — **QUEEN of WANDS.** — **KING of WANDS**

Adventure, excitement, enthusiasm	Bravery, energetic, hot-tempered	Self-assuredness, charisma, passion	Leadership, vision, taking control

Example of a Reading ❧ *Client No 4601- Shania*
Will I find my true-life partner in 2024?
Feedback: 100% correct. Thank you for the insight, not just a
prediction. I didn't think of it this way. Look forward to meeting
my Knight of Pentacles!

QUEEN of CUPS.	Past	THE DEVIL.	KNIGHT of PENTACLES
Personality	Past	Present	Future Possibilities
Highly intuitive, compassionate and loving nature	Heartbreak, three past relationships	Shadow self, nursing past grievances	Loyal & secure relationship

The Three of Swords is the heartbreak you have suffered in the past. Three relationships that have not worked out. The Three of Swords depicts the message of rejection, betrayal, hurt and discouragement. Suffering is meant to make us stronger, more careful and more vigilant.

Most fear the card of **the Devil**. However, this should not be the case. He appears here just to ask you to pay heed to what the psyche may bring up at the time.

The Devil card represents your shadow (or darker) side and the negative forces that constrain you and hold you back from being the best version of yourself. The Devil card often appears when you have been tricked into thinking you have no control over your shadow self or these negative forces, and that you can never break free from their hold.

It may be a recurring pattern for you, and it will take a tremendous amount of willpower and strength to free yourself from their influence.

When The Devil shows up in a Tarot reading, see it as an opportunity to bring these negative influences into your conscious awareness, so you can then act to free yourself from their hold. Shine your light on the negative patterns that have been standing in your way for so long, and over time, you will loosen the grip they have on you.

Given that The Devil is a Major Arcana card, it is unlikely that you will be free from them overnight. However, take the advice of the cards that appeared before dear Shania, and you will come through to healing yourself and becoming whole. This I know.

The Knight of Pentacles is coming into your life! He is patient, reliable and steady. He would be a trustworthy and dedicated partner, a bit stubborn as it is difficult to get him to change his mind, but in a relationship both of you will work towards your long-term goals together.

Your personality as the **Queen of Cups** is very intuitive and compassionate. Listen to your Higher Self which is your intuition and banish the Devil and your shadow self.

Hurts and grievances from past relationships need to be healed and let go, or they will repeat their patterns in your future.

What lessons were learnt?

Effective communication is very important in a relationship. I feel you need to communicate and be vulnerable in your relationships.

The Knight of Pentacles is coming. The Tarot predicts future possibilities. However, it is up to you to work on yourself *now* and develop the relationship with your true-life partner which is in your future possibility.

You create what you desire.

Day Four

The 3R's

Routines

Relationships

Responsibilities

The Formula

My specific formula … let's go! Yes, it works, tried and tested. Believe me and have faith!

Keep connected with the Tarot. Each day, practice a little self-care in your way. Whether it is prayer, meditation, walking in nature, or a massage – just spend some time with your cards, asking the Universe and your guides to connect to you in a quiet space and time.

Rider Waite Tarot Deck	Spread Sheet & Tote Bag	Crystals	Sage	Sacred Space

Let's begin your first reading: You learn by doing. This has been my way, to put the cart before the horse as it were and jump in when you know enough – not everything!

For this mini course, we are going to only use upright cards. You may wish to go on to reading reversed cards yourself at a later stage.

There are many interpretations of the reversed Tarot cards in books and on the internet to avail yourself of. In this mini course, we are working with the traditional Rider Waite deck of cards. I still work with this deck which is bright and colourful and has a lot of pictorial detail for developing intuition I feel.

I will share my secret. To this day I prefer to read upright cards only. For myself and others.

Why?

My natural way of thinking is that there is nothing negative happening to me. The Universe does not dish out negative happenings to some and favourable things to others.

We create what we experience.

They are just the lessons we need to learn. Repetition occurs in different ways if we don't pay heed and look for the lesson in the "negative" experience we get. Which we have created in the first place because we are heading the wrong way down our path or towards a goal we want to accomplish.

Prepare your space.

Make your sacred space personal. Choose the looks and feels that resonate with you. Choose objects that give you energy and inspire you or help you to get fully immersed in your sacred practice of Tarot.

If you have a whole room to dedicate to your sacred space, you are fortunate. However, if not, use a screen or curtain or other boundary to make your sacred space feel contained, relaxing and personal to meditate, manifest and commune with the divine.

In the early days of my spiritual journey, I used to collect objects, crystals and gemstones, statues and magical wands for my sacred space. Nowadays, the sacred lives in my thoughts and feelings all the time. Spirituality is an evolution, and the Universe will reveal the next step for you in your own journey. Allow your spiritual practice to change and evolve over time just as you do.

A fancy Tarot spread cloth is not necessary. Use any cloth you like to create the space for the reading. Just keep it separate in a draw or box with your cards for your readings.

Sage is the best herb to burn to dispel any negativity before a reading. Sage sticks are quite inexpensive or burn a few dry sage leaves from a pot grown in your garden, in a bowl, and pass your cards through the smoke. Pluck a few leaves from the sage plant and keep them with your Tarot cards. The cards can live in a tote bag or box or just wrapped in the spread cloth.

Crystals are wonderful to bring in energy. Choose a couple of your choice. Amethyst and Rose quartz are good for healing and love energy. A **lit-up candle** radiates powerful, yet soft and positive energy. **Music** that dispels negative energy I find is wonderful. I have Tibetan bowl music which I play during each reading. You can download this from the internet for free on YouTube. This is the one I use:
https://www.youtube.com/watch?v=x6UlTRjhijl. You can download it onto your computer without the advertisements.

Spend a moment or two in silence asking the Universe or whoever you feel connected to, a special angelic presence or spiritual energy, to help you. I am not religious, but I have a connection with Archangel Michael through the Ace of Swords.

Personality · Past · Present · Future Guidance

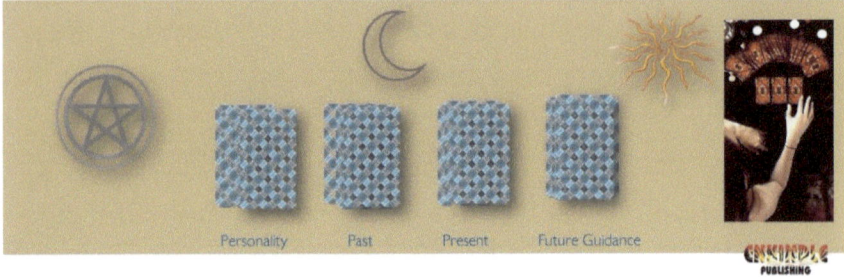

Think of your question. Better still, write it down.

- Shuffle. Divide the deck into 4 piles. Not necessary to be even, or tidy!
- Pick one card from the top of each pile. Lay them out on your spread cloth in the order of Personality . Past . Present . Future
- Meditate on each and jot down what YOU see in each card.

The cheat sheet I have done for you is at your side. Try and use your own intuition as well as glance at my sheet and see what else

YOU see in the card. The more you work on your intuition, the faster it will develop for you. (You can download the Intuition Guide from my website https://stephanieroberts.college under "Intuitive Tarot for Women" Cheat Sheet.)

Trust it. Believe in it.

You know your past and your present. But just look at the definition the card gives you. I can tell you YOU, will be surprised! Put the ego aside. You will advance in leaps and bounds. This is where the magic starts to happen!!

Go back and look at the Example Reading to help you interpret your reading. I don't mean it will be the same in any way, but the method of interpretation will guide you while you are a newbie.

Stephanie Marie

Author and Tarot Advisor
Enkindle Publishing
Creator of "Intuitive Tarot for Women" a Simple Mini Course

Facebook:
https://www.facebook.com/StephanieRobertsTeacher
https://www.facebook.com/StephanieRobertsWriter
https://www.facebook.com/StephanieRobertsAuthor/

Website:
https://stephanieroberts.college

Udemy:
https://www.udemy.com/user/stephanie-roberts-18/

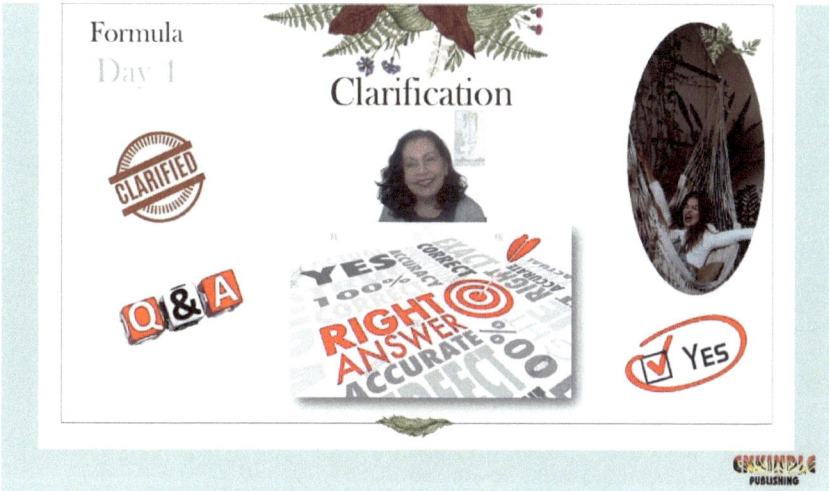

When I started, and still to this day, I use a clarification card for every reading before I present it to the client.

By this I mean choose a card that resonates with you and positive energy from the deck which will always stay as your clarification card. My card is *Ace of Swords* (Mental Clarity, Clear Thinking, Breakthroughs, Ability To Concentrate, Communication, Realising The Truth, Vision, Force, Focus – all through The White Light and Archangel Michael for confirmation and clarification).

We will use your clarification card at the end of the reading. You will get to have a close union with your confirmation card!

How do you do this? Go back to the pictures of the 78 cards. Which card attracts you? Which card is calling to you? What is your focus in life? Pick ONE card accordingly from the Suit. *Choose carefully* as this card will stay with you as your clarification for your readings. Your guides will clarify through this card when you state it as your clarification and confirmation card.

I like to have a spreadsheet. Choose or make one if you can sew. My spreadsheet silk cloth is printed with the Ace of Swords, my clarification card. However, you don't have to have one to do a reading. This just creates a nice space for your cards. Printed silk spreadsheets can be ordered from outlets on the internet if you wish to have one.

Lay out your four cards and complete your intuitive reading. Please trust yourself. Just go with what comes up.

Remember you are reading YOUR life. Put the ego aside. What do the cards want to tell you?

The Tarot always tells us what we need to know to get where we want to go.

- *What lessons are brought up from the past?*
- *Are you repeating the same mistakes of the past in the present?*
- *Future is a prediction of what can happen in your life if you address your past, change things in your present to create what the Universe wants you to create in your future **to get what you want**!*

Remember the Tarot predicts your future possibilities – YOU create it.

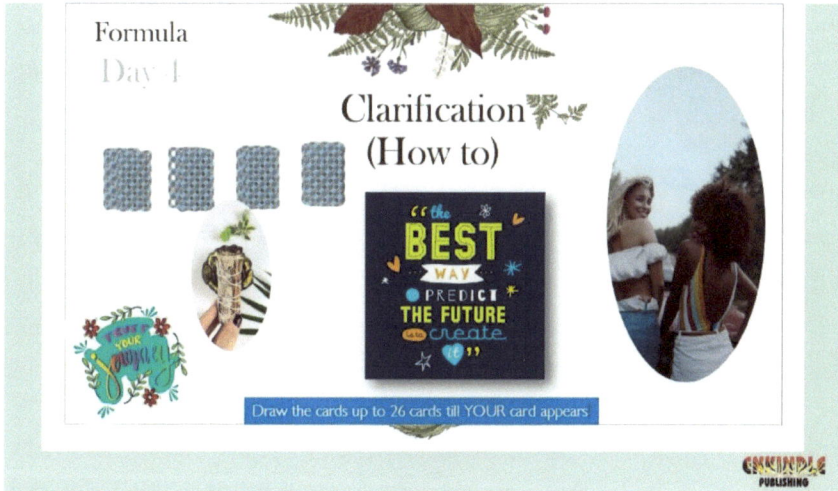

Clarification
(How to)

"the
BEST
WAY
PREDICT
THE FUTURE
create"

Draw the cards up to 26 cards till YOUR card appears

When you have interpreted your four cards, we are going to confirm the reading with our Clarification Card.

Don't doubt. You will find as you read for yourself, this Card will be your best friend and guide. You will learn to trust this Card and your developing INTUITION. Till you completely trust it, when things start panning out. That is if you do the WORK!

Question you may ask –
Q. Do I leave the four cards drawn on the spread or put them back in the deck?

A. Leave the four cards of the reading on the spread cloth. Just shuffle the rest of the cards.

If it just so happens that your Clarification Card is amongst the four cards read – put it back in the deck.

Pass the pack of cards through the Sage Smoke.

Shuffle. Lay out four piles of cards again. Close your eyes and tap into your intuition, asking your guide to come in to confirm that the reading is correct.

Start picking the cards. One from each pile. Keep going till you have counted 26 cards. Your clarification card will come up for you within that number. Immediately at card 1 and sometimes in-between or right at the end. Why the number of 26. This is one-third of the pack of 78 cards.

Don't worry if it does not at first. Go back to your reading and look carefully at it again. Are you working from the heart not from the ego? There is something that you may have missed. Add it to your written reading.

Pass the cards through the Sage Smoke. *Clarify again.*

You may have to repeat this at least 3 times when you are beginning to use intuition. Don't give up. It works 100%!

Mastery

Finally, on to Mastery of your own intuition and your Tarot cards! How exciting! Keep the faith going. Believe in yourself and your intuition.

Remember no-one is perfect. I would not be where I am today if I was only seeking perfection and getting disheartened because I wasn't becoming perfect. Take IMPERFECT ACTION.

Learn as you go, about YOURSELF, LIFE, and the TAROT.

How we get there

Memorize the Basics ONLY 🌙   Develop Intuition ✋   Read Clarify and Confirm ✓ 💡

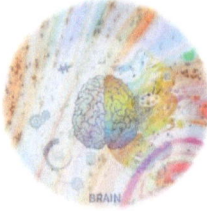

Memorize the Basics only:

- the 78 Cards divided into the 21 Major Arcana + The Fool (The Journeyer)
- the 3 Realms of the Major Arcana
- the Minor Arcana divided into the Four Suits

Develop Intuition:

- my Cheat Sheet is for your guidance, till you start seeing visions in the cards from your own intuition, pertaining to your circumstances. You will. Remember to go with your first impression. Don't doubt. Don't let Ego step-in.

Clarify and Confirm:

› You have chosen your Clarifier.
  Don't change it. You will form a relationship with this card. Go by how you feel when you select the confirmation card. It will appear within the
  first 26 Card pick from the pack. No. 1 – in- between – or at card 26.

Ask your guidance before you draw cards. Thank your guidance when the cards appears.

If it doesn't when you first start reading. Don't worry. Go back and look at your four-card draw and interpret some more.

DO NOT change the DRAW of Four Cards! Repeat the confirmation.

- Believe.
- Trust.
- Ask for
  Guidance.

Tip: I prefer not to let others handle my cards. The energy remains strong within my aura. I sleep with them under my pillow at night to absorb the energy of the Universe and mine. This works for me. It may work for you too!

Cleanse your cards regularly by passing them through Sage smoke. I find this is the most effective way for me. Selenite is a powerful healing crystal that promotes peace and calm, mental clarity, and well-being. This crystal can remove negative energy and help you connect to higher realms. Keep Selenite with your cards to cleanse.

The best way I can describe the experience of having a followup reading with Stephanie is to liken it to a follow-up visit with your doctor. In the initial visit, you were provided with some diagnostic information and some guidance as to what course of action is likely to result in the outcome you desire, and a bit of information about what that future outcome might look like. At the follow-up, you are faced with the results of your efforts and choices since that guidance.

In my case the follow-up had incredibly positive results. Now, if you are reading this review, I realize that you don't know me, and my results may be of little interest. But the reason I tell you this is as follows: *An initial reading with Stephanie will diagnose your past and present. It will show you potential outcomes for your future, the future you are desiring to build for yourself. It will also give you guidance as to the internal and external work that needs to be done in order to achieve the life you long for.*

This is where you come in. If you have an open heart and an open mind and truly do take the guidance in and do the work, you can progress at a rapid pace. A short time later, I highly recommend that you come in for a follow-up reading. Check in and see how your work is progressing you toward the goal and if needed, find out how you might need to adjust to get to where you are trying to go.

Stephanie's readings are intuitive, insightful, and she has a heart to help others. She truly has the ability to be a valuable part of your team, and if you are willing to accept guidance and do the work, she can help you progress rapidly toward your goals. *I, for one, have been doing the work, and my follow-up has shown that I am progressing rapidly toward the life I am truly designing for myself.*

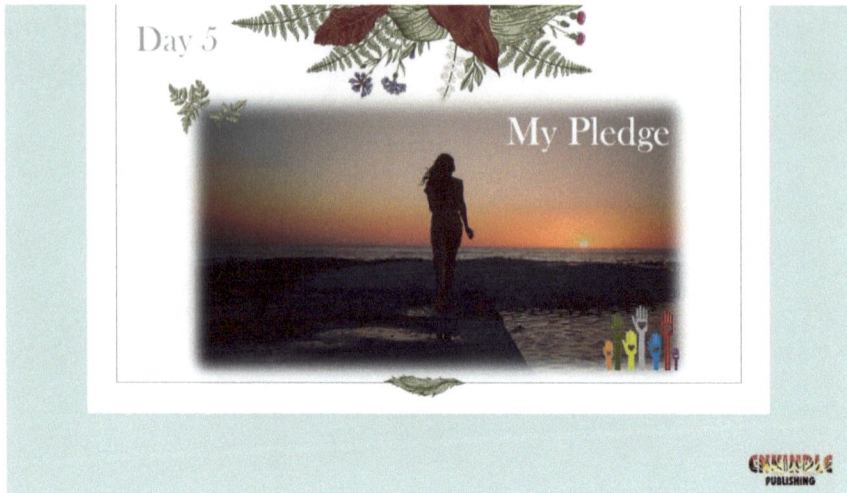

At *Enkindle Publishing* I believe in giving 110%. By giving back, our own lives move forward in leaps and bounds in abundance. We help others thrive as we grow ourselves.

To all my students enrolled in this course you are welcome to my knowledge, advice and counsel through the Tarot as you develop your intuitive skills, move forward, and create the **Life of Your Dreams!**

Just drop me a line at: info@stephanieroberts.college

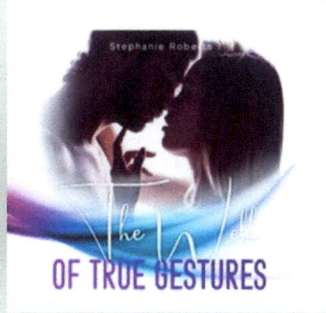

Day 5

A Big
THANK
YOU!

Stephanie Marie Roberts

https://stephanieroberts.college
https://www.facebook.com/StephanieRobertsWriter
https://www.facebook.com/StephanieRobertsAuthor
https://www.facebook.com/StephanieRobertsTeacher

Thank you so much for joining me in this mini-Tarot course.

I wish you much love and light in your journey forward.

Stay connected. I am always there for you. Stephanie ♍.

Please leave a review on Amazon under the purchase of this eBook. I would appreciate it.

About the Author

OM MANI PADME HUM

Om Mani Padme Hum is a traditional Buddhist mantra that is believed to have a therapeutic effect on the mind and body. The mantra is believed to evoke compassion and wisdom, and to purify negative karma and negative emotions.

Stephanie Marie Roberts' love of writing has found a vibrant expression in illustrated children's books. Her journey as an author began with a simple yet profound desire to bring joy to her little grandsons, Joshua, Liam, and Nicky. What started as personal tales for her grandchildren blossomed into a passion for creating enchanting stories for children around the globe.

Stephanie's talent and dedication to her craft have been recognized through prestigious accolades. She is a proud recipient of the Book Excellence Literary Award and a Silver Medallist for her beloved books, "Liam Shark Boy" and "Joshua's World". These stories captivate young readers with their whimsical illustrations and heartwarming narratives.

Her literary repertoire extends beyond these award-winning titles. "Nicky Superhero" is a delightful tale embodying lessons in kindness and encouragement, inspiring children to embrace their inner hero. Meanwhile, "Billie Red Wattle Bird" is a charming story that imparts valuable lessons about responsibility and highlights the beauty of the Australian flora and fauna.

Stephanie's creative talents are not confined to children's literature alone. An incurable romantic at heart, she has also penned the touching fiction novel, "Always". This tear-jerking story draws from her own life experiences in the fifties and seventies, offering readers a poignant glimpse into a bygone era.

As Stephanie embarks on the final chapter of her life's narrative, she continues to define herself as a multifaceted writer. Her interests have expanded to encompass holistic studies. Her eLearning courses on Udemy are complemented by her insightful books, "Gain Insight to Read Tarot for Yourself in 5 Days – Intuitive Tarot for Women" and "Healthy Relationships – The Well of True Gestures". These works serve as invaluable companions for those seeking to deepen their understanding of the Tarot and foster Healthy Relationships.

For those eager to delve into Stephanie's enchanting world of storytelling and holistic wisdom, her works can be found on her website and on Udemy. Stephanie Marie Roberts' journey as an author is a testament to her boundless creativity, her love for sharing stories, and her commitment to guiding others on their paths to self-discovery.

www.ingramcontent.com/pod-product-compliance
Lightning Source LLC
Chambersburg PA
CBHW041357090426
42739CB00001B/3